VEGETABLE JAPAN COOKBOOK

50 Recipes for Greens and Plant Based Dishes from Japan

Maya Zein

© **Copyright 2021 by Maya Zein - All rights reserved.**

This document is geared towards providing exact and reliable information in regards to the topic and issue covered. The publication is sold with the idea that the publisher is not required to render accounting, officially permitted, or otherwise, qualified services. If advice is necessary, legal or professional, a practiced individual in the profession should be ordered.

- From a Declaration of Principles which was accepted and approved equally by a Committee of the American Bar Association and a Committee of Publishers and Associations.

It is not legal in any way to reproduce, duplicate, or transmit any part of this document in either electronic means or in printed format. Recording of this publication is strictly prohibited and any storage of this document is not allowed unless with written permission from the publisher. All rights reserved.

The information provided herein is stated to be truthful and consistent, in that any liability, in terms of inattention or otherwise, by any usage or abuse of any policies, processes, or directions contained within is the solitary and utter responsibility of the recipient reader. Under no circumstances will any legal responsibility or blame be held against the publisher for any reparation, damages, or monetary loss due to the information herein, either directly or indirectly.

Respective authors own all copyrights not held by the publisher.

The information herein is offered for informational purposes solely, and is universal as so. The presentation of the information is without contract or any type of guarantee assurance.

The trademarks that are used are without any consent, and the publication of the trademark is without permission or backing by the trademark owner. All trademarks and brands within this book are for clarifying purposes only and are the owned by the owners themselves, not affiliated with this document.

Contents

INTRODUCTION 7

CHAPTER 1: VEGETARIAN JAPANESE APPETIZERS AND BREAKFAST RECIPES.................................10

1.1 Teriyaki Mushroom Bowls 10

1.2 Japanese Rice Balls 12

1.3 Japanese Breakfast Porridge Bowl 15

1.4 Tofu Hiyayakko 16

1.5 Tamagoyaki Scramble 18

1.6 Macrobiotic Pearled Barley Ojiya 20

1.7 Tamago Kake Gohan 21

1.8 Japanese Natto 23

1.9 Vegetable Gyoza 25

1.10 Salmon Cucumber Tartare Bites............................27

1.11 Pancakes Dorayaki..29

1.12 Japanese Ogura Toast 31

1.13 Vegetable Lo Mein..32

CHAPTER 2: VEGETARIAN JAPANESE LUNCH AND DINNER RECIPES 34

2.1 Vegetarian Ramen 34

2.2 Japanese Mitarashi Dango 36

2.3 Vegetarian Okonomiyaki 38

2.4 Japanese Soba Noodles 39

2.5 Soy-Glazed Eggplant Donburi 41

2.6 Spicy Tofu Bento Bowl 43

2.7 Japanese Rice Balls with Avocado Filling and Sweet Potato 44

2.8 Lightly Fried Japanese Vegetables 46

2.9 Tofu Yasai Don 47

2.10 Yasai Itame 51

2.11 Cucumber Sunomono 53

2.12 Mashed Tofu Salad with Green Bean 55

2.13 Japanese Rice Balls with Avocado Filling 56

2.14 Yakitori Grilled Skewers 58

2.15 Vegetable Yakisoba 60

2.16 Japanese Fruit Sandwich 62

CHAPTER 3: VEGETARIAN JAPANESE SNACK, SOUPS, AND SALAD RECIPES 64

3.1 Miso Soup with Tofu, Wakame Seaweed 64

3.2 Creamy Miso Pasta with Tofu and Asparagus 66

3.3 Green Bean Shiraae (Mashed Tofu Salad with Green Bean)68

3.4 Tofu Katsu with Spicy Sweet-Sour Sauce 70

3.5 Vegetarian Katsu Curry 72

3.6 Somen Noodles with Nori Dressing 73

3.7 15-Minute Miso Soup with Greens and Tofu 74

3.8 Kenchin Vegetable Soup 76

3.9 Hearty Vegetable Miso Soup... 78

3.10 Japanese Vegetable Stew with Miso Broth...................... 79

3.11 Homemade Senbei Rice Crackers 81

CHAPTER 4: JAPANESE VEGAN RECIPES 83

4.1 Homemade Vegan Sushi Recipe 83

4.2 Vegan Japanese Souffle Pancakes 85

4.3 Japanese Vegan Pancakes Dorayaki with Red Bean Filling 87

4.4 Vegan Poke Bowl... 89

4.5 Japanese Vegan Udon Noodle Soup 92

4.6 Vegan Nabe (Hot Pot with Miso) 94

4.7 Japanese-Style Katsudon Rice Bowls 96

4.8 Japanese Coco Ichibanya-Style Vegetable Curry............. 99

4.9 Spicy Vegetarian Ramen Gyoza....................................... 101

4.10 Japanese Miso Eggplant... 102

CONCLUSION.. 104

Introduction

Japan has a long tradition of veganism, except for seafood, mostly consumed raw as seafood or sushi, thanks to its Buddhist origins. In the early 1900s, Japan's diet started to change with beef and foreign cooking methods. Perfect presentation, tasty flavors, and healthy fresh ingredients are the hallmarks of Japanese cuisine. The flavor of the fish is extremely important. Seasonality is also important whenever it comes to vegetables. As a result, the two important key values of Japanese food are flavor and variability. The third main quality of Japanese cuisine is elegance.

Seasonal veggies are cleaned and gently cooked in liquid to bring out their delicate flavor. Also, dishes that take a long time to prepare are, on the whole, pleasing to the palate. Another loved product is processed soybeans, which come from white miso, red miso, and sesame oil, which are used in condiments, sauces, and spice mixes. Tonkatsu is based on a Viennese schnitzel and miso, which utilizes the European process of smashing and deep-frying, which are now part of modern Japanese cuisine. Japanese cuisine refers to the country's ethnic and cultural foods, which have evolved through decades of political, technological, and cultural progress. The standard Japanese cuisine consists of rice, fried rice, and other foods, focusing on new flavors.

In Europe, dairy products are not as common as they are in Japan. Between the ninth and fourteenth centuries, the first Japanese milk product known to the world was developed. Livestock was often developed solely to pull carts or plow fields.It was a long-forgotten tradition to use them for beef or even dairy until lately. Using them for beef or even milk was a farfetched tradition until quite recently.

Japanese food has taken the horticultural environment by storm. With its unique flavorings and a sensitive mixture of salty and sweet, it is no wonder Japanese ingredients are so common. From ramen to sushi, dishes influenced by Japanese and Japanese could be seen anywhere, such as your country's restaurants! To take home the magnificent Japanese food ingredients, you do not need to be a professional chef.

Each food is named "Gohan." by the Japanese. For instance, breakfast is called "asa-Gohan." In traditional Japanese dishes, a cup of boiled rice is also included and may be a component of dinner, breakfast, or lunch. The side dishes are known as okazu and are eaten with broth and rice. While Japan is a small world, each area and even town has its distinct flavor. Food from the Kanto areas (the eastern part of the big island) and the Kansai area (the western part of the big island) are the most popular. Kanto cuisine is known for its bold flavors, while Kansai cuisine is known for its soft seasoning. Many dishes in the Kansai and Kanto areas are prepared differently. Traditional Japanese meals involve a cup of fried rice, which can be eaten for breakfast, noon, or supper.

The Japanese diet is focused on long-term health philosophy. Japanese cuisine is not only delicious and enticing, but it also has several health advantages. Uncooked meats, added sugars or foods, and many fruit and legumes are all part of traditional Japanese cuisine. Hormone-dependent tumors, such as breast and cervical cancer, have historically been rare in Japan. This is due to a higher intake of vegetables, berries, good fats, high-fiber products, and a lower calorie consumption. Japan has one of the lowest levels of cardiovascular disease development globally and even lower compared to developing countries.

The Japanese diet is full of foods that help support heart health, which explains why there are very few cases of heart disease. Green tea, which has various health benefits, is commonly served with Japanese dishes. Green tea has been shown to help lower blood pressure, strengthen the immune system, lower blood pressure, and delay the aging process.

Japanese food is associated with better food and has a deep relationship with the region's long-expected lifespan. One of the key factors behind all this is 'ichijyusansa' that applies to a meal composed of brown rice and broth, the main dish of fish or meat, and a fresh salad of vegetables or seaweed all slightly flavored to display the components' natural flavors. With these extinct flavors, "Vegetarian Japanese Cookbook" has a wide range of delicious Japanese vegetarian recipes. It has four chapters with appetizers, snacks, breakfast, lunch, dinner, desserts, and Japan's most famous vegan recipes. Read this book, follow these recipes, and have a flavorful, delicious meal every day.

Chapter 1: Vegetarian Japanese Appetizers and Breakfast Recipes

1.1 Teriyaki Mushroom Bowls

This meal gets a boost of umami flavor from these roasted mushrooms. A fast and simple vegetarian midweek supper in these flavorful, Japanese-inspired teriyaki mushrooms with rice. It features a savory coating prepared with soy sauce, mirin (Japanese rice wine), and syrup. It also depends on intense heat, normally provided by a broiler or grill, to get that delicious flavor. They are light, healthful, and satisfying, and they only need one pan. Mushrooms are one of the greatest veggie alternatives for meat, whether you are vegan or vegetarian or simply aiming to eat a few more vegetarian meals each week. They have a meaty feel and are naturally high in umami. Fill your dish with your preferred grain (white rice works well here), top on the mushrooms, broccoli, and any additional vegetables you choose! It is fully vegan, and by adding tamari, you can keep it gluten-free!

Cooking Time: 45 minutes

Serving Size: 4

Ingredients:

- 2 tablespoon sesame seeds
- 2-3 scallions, sliced thinly
- 1 teaspoon red chili flakes
- 1 lb. broccolini, about 12 stalks
- 1 cup dry brown rice
- 2 garlic cloves, finely minced
- 2 teaspoon ginger, minced

- 6 Portobello mushrooms
- 1 tablespoon white miso paste
- 1 tablespoon brown sugar
- 3 tablespoon soy sauce
- 2 tablespoon rice vinegar
- 3 tablespoon sesame oil

Method:
1. Heat the flame to 425 degrees F.
2. Slice the mushrooms and cover them with 1 tablespoon of sesame oil.
3. Switch to a cookie dish and bake until the mushroom is soft and the liquid flows for twenty minutes, rotating halfway across.
4. Cook rice as per the instructions in the box.
5. In the meantime, in a small shallow saucepan, mix the brown sugar, rice vinegar, soy sauce, ginger, garlic, and chili powder.
6. Heat till the sugar dissolves, and the paste gets thicker into a coating, stirring regularly.
7. Pull them from the cooker until the mushroom is baked.
8. With both the teriyaki coating, coat all parts of the mushroom and the red cabbage.
9. Spray with sesame oil and clear everything from the cooker.
10. For a side dish, serve broccoli and mushroom over rice and finish with spring onions.

1.2 Japanese Rice Balls

The Japanese rice ball, commonly known as onigiri, is a perfect illustration of how imaginative Japanese food can be. Onigiri is a Japanese rice ball prepared with cooked or heated sushi rice, furikake spices (and sometimes delectable secret ingredients), and enveloped in nori seaweed. They are either cooked at home or bought at a local Konbini (convenience shop) in Japan and then carried to school or work as a pleasant snack or fast lunch. It is also a Japanese comfort meal made from steamed rice covered in nori and shaped into a triangle, spherical, or cylinder form (dried seaweed). Onigiri is comparable to sushi rolls but not the same as hand-rolled temaki sushi. The most significant distinction is that traditional sushi is flavored with sushi vinegar, while onigiri originates with sticky rice.

Cooking Time: 1 hour

Serving Size: 4

Ingredients:

- 1 teaspoon toasted sesame oil
- ½ avocado
- ½ teaspoon salt
- ½ – 1 small sweet potato
- 2 tablespoon rice wine vinegar
- 1 tablespoon sugar
- 3 cups water
- ¼ cup sesame seeds
- 1 ½ cup brown sushi rice

Teriyaki Sauce

- 2 tablespoons sugar

- 1 tablespoon rice wine vinegar
- 5 tablespoons soy sauce
- 5 tablespoons mirin
- Vegetable oil for frying

Method:

1. Begin by doing the rice cleaning.
2. Quantify the rice into the pan and wash it with cool water several times till the water no longer looks murky and begins to appear clean. Drain some rice.
3. Use ice water to coat the rice, put the pot on the flame, and protect it with a cover. Switch the heat off when the water heats.
4. Offer it a stirring and allow the water to consume the rice.
5. The rice must be weak after thirty minutes. Drain all water in bulk.
6. Strip a large mixing bowl with films from the kitchen and drop around one tablespoon of cooled rice in it.
7. Preheat the frying pan and pour some oil over it.
8. Fry Onigiri over medium temperature until crisp and well caramelized, three minutes per hand. Serve with teriyaki sauce instantly.
9. Integrate the soya sauce, vinegar, mirin, and sugar in a shallow saucepan.
10. Bring it to a boil with the gravy. Blend the corn starch with liquid in a tiny cup.
11. Steadily dump the corn starch combination into the sauce when continuously stirring it.

12. Continue cooking until you have caramelized the sauce. Switch the heat off over the pan.

1.3 Japanese Breakfast Porridge Bowl

It is a bowl of straightforward rice and watermeal. In a saucepan with water, the rice is cooked until it collapses. In Japan, rice is regarded as a healing meal since it is sensitive, soft, and readily digested. People who are recuperating from illness, the elderly, or newborns are generally served Okayu. Some variations include protein and a variety of toppings, making them ideal for lunch or supper.

Contrary to popular belief, the Japanese do not consume porridge as a normal meal regularly as the Chinese. Okayu, on the other hand, is provided as a therapeutic dish designed to calm the body and replenish vitality. Because the toppings are minimal, the dish itself is light and moderate in flavor.

Cooking Time: 10 minutes

Serving Size: 1

Ingredients:

- 20g of firm
- Water for desired consistency
- 1 tablespoon nutritional yeast
- ¼ of a small avocado
- 20g round brown rice (dry)
- 1 nori sheet, shredded
- 1 teaspoon miso paste
- ½ cup chopped leek
- 20g rolled oats

To Garnish

- Sesame seeds
- Paprika powder

Method:
1. Begin by draining brown rice. Wash and clean.
2. Place the rolled oats in a shallow saucepan in the morning before preparing the porridge, adding only enough hot water to fill them. Just put it aside.
3. You could either rip the nori papers with your palms or cut them with knives.
4. Then, cook the soaked rice and the sliced leek in a room temperature water frying pan till the rice is ready, about ten minutes.
5. Turn the heating off. Then, blend in the soaking rolled oats and insert the appropriate boiling water.
6. Then, combine some liquid with miso paste and switch things up with ripped nori paper and nutritional yeast into the mixture.
7. Again, when necessary, add a little water.

1.4 Tofu Hiyayakko

It is cold tofu from Japan that is offered as an appetizer or side dish. The tofu's silky, smooth, and creamy texture helps to chill the body and welcomes relief on a hot day. It is a classic midsummer meal to offer with Edamame. Hiyayakko is made from silken tofu, which has a softer and velvety texture than ordinary tofu. Because silken tofu contains a lot more moisture, it must be drained for 10-15 minutes before serving. Take a brief look at the meal before bringing it to the table. If any water seems to be escaping from the tofu, gently tilt the presentation platter and pour it off.

Cooking Time: 10 minutes

Serving Size: 1

Ingredients:

- 1 pinch bonito shavings
- 1 pinch toasted sesame seeds
- 1 ½ teaspoon fresh ginger root
- ¼ teaspoon green onion
- 1 tablespoon soy sauce
- ½ teaspoon water
- ¼ (12 ounces) package silken tofu
- ½ teaspoon dashi granules
- 1 teaspoon white sugar

Method:

1. In a shallow bowl, blend the sugar, dashi granules, soy sauce, and water when the sugar is dissolved.
2. On a small dish, put the tofu and cover it with green onion, ginger, and bonito granules.

3. Sprinkle on top of the soy combination and scatter with sesame seeds.

1.5 Tamagoyaki Scramble

Tamagoyaki is a traditional omelet wrapped up and flavored with mirin, sesame oil, and sugar. Tamago signifies eggs in Japanese, while yaki indicates grill. Tamagoyaki, or wrapped eggs, comes in various forms in Japanese food, which might be bewildering. Tamagoyaki has a somewhat sweet flavor and a custardy consistency that appeals to both children and adults in Japan. Over rice, this tamagoyaki omelet is sweet, savory, soft, and delectable. Tamagoyaki is deceptively tough to produce because of its artistic appearance. The process entails rolling tiny omelets carefully and folding them into a stacked log, which is then cut.

Cooking Time: 3 minutes

Serving Size: 1

Ingredients:

- ¼ teaspoon black salt
- pepper to taste
- 2 teaspoon sugar (10g)
- ⅛ teaspoon baking powder
- ½ teaspoon kombu dashi
- 2 teaspoon mirin (10g)
- 1 sheet yuba
- 3 tablespoon liquid of choice
- 1 teaspoon soy sauce
- ¼ cup silken tofu (60g)

Garnish

- Scallions
- Sesame seeds
- Kizami nori
- Soy sauce

Optional
- 1 tablespoon vegan kewpie mayo
- Pinch of turmeric
- 2 teaspoon nutritional yeast (8g)

Method:
1. Moisturize in warm water for 3-5 minutes, dry yuba.
2. Rip the yuba into smaller parts, about around the size of a fist.
3. Mix soy milk, silken tofu, mirin, soy sauce, rice, dashi, sugar, and baking powder thoroughly.
4. This is going to be the eggy mixture, which shuffles as well.
5. Over medium-high heat, warm a bowl, and add oils or vegetarian butter.
6. Add the silken tofu and put the yuba stuff on top. Before handling it, let it cook for around two minutes.
7. Use spoons or a spatula until the sides start to look fried, then force the sides into the center.
8. Lower the heat and simmer for another thirty seconds, moving the egg mixture to the right texture every few minutes.
9. Squeeze the black salt on edge using your fingertips.

10. Take it out of the oven and eat on the sides or over pasta.

1.6 Macrobiotic Pearled Barley Ojiya

A typical morning meal is ojiya, Japanese-style flavored oatmeal with veggies. Usually, rice is used, but flaked barley should be used instead in this vegan meal. Miso, onions, beets, celery, and scallions are used for cooking the grains. It is ideal for cold mornings when you want something hearty to eat. It features a savory coating prepared with soy sauce, mirin (Japanese rice wine), and a sweetener. It also depends on intense heat, normally provided by a broiler or grill, to get that delicious flavor.

Cooking Time: 35 minutes

Serving Size: 3

Ingredients:

For the Pearled Barley

- A pinch of sea salt
- 1 cup pearled barley

For the Ojiya

- ½-1 tablespoon barley miso
- Scallions, for garnish
- 2 tablespoons diced celery
- 1 tablespoon sliced leek
- 1 cup cooked pearled barley
- 2 tablespoons diced carrots
- ¼ cup diced onion

Method:

1. Place the pearled barley in a frying pan with the soaking water and kosher salt.
2. Bring to the boil, seal, minimize medium heat, and steam for 45-50 minutes.
3. Take from the fire and leave to steam for ten minutes or sit. Balance the cooked grains softly.
4. In a small saucepan, put cooked pearled grain and 2/3 of a cup of hot water and bring to a boil.
5. Add the carrots, onions, celery, and leek. Cover and cook for ten minutes or until the vegetables are tender.
6. Add a little liquid if you like a soupier texture and boil until it becomes soft.
7. Decrease the heat to a low level and insert a small liquid volume to melt the miso in a shallow bowl.
8. To the bowl, insert miso. If required, change the taste. For five more minutes, continue simmering.
9. Serve hot with your choice of dressings.

1.7 Tamago Kake Gohan

Tamago Gohan (meaning "egg rice") is a basic Japanese comfort dish made with rice and a raw egg. That is one of my all-time favorite recipes, and it just takes a few minutes to prepare. It is a substantial and tasty breakfast or late-night meal that can be thrown together in minutes. Begin with a bowl of rice—you will need roughly a cup of boiled rice per egg. It may be cold, moderate, warm, or wherever in between as it isn't stale. If you have leftover rice, put it in a dish, top it with a plate, and heat it for a minute. Creating a small well in the rice assists a little, and it is also attractive, but it is by no means required.

Cooking Time: 50 minutes

Serving Size: 2

Ingredients:

- 1 scallion, finely chopped
- Sesame seeds, for sprinkling
- Extra-virgin olive oil
- 2 eggs
- Splashes of tamari
- 3 cups cooked brown rice

Method:

1. Squeeze out two cups of fried brown rice.
2. Put 1 egg per cup alongside splatters of tamari when the rice is boiling; mix rapidly so that the egg heats softly while the rice covers, giving the rice a creamy texture.
3. Cover each cup with spring onions, pumpkin seeds, and the extra toppings you want. Serve on the surface with miso for flavor.

1.8 Japanese Natto

Natto is a Traditional Japanese meal prepared from fermented soybeans and Bacillus subtilis var. natto bacteria. It is often offered during breakfast. It is usually accompanied with karoshi dijon, soya or sake sauce, and Japanese bunching onions. Because of its pungent odor, pungent flavor, and sticky, slimy consistency, natto is frequently considered an addictive stimulant. This fermented dish has a distinct consistency and aroma. Many people believe it is an acquired taste. This should not, however, discourage you. Natto is high in nutrients and has been linked to various health advantages, including denser muscles, a better heart, and a healthy immune system. Natto has lower levels of vitamin B6, folic, and pantothenic, as well as enzymes and other helpful plant components. One of these advantages is that it makes meals more digestible, making it simpler for your stomach to collect their nutrients.

Cooking Time: 5 minutes

Serving Size: 1

Ingredients:

- 1 teaspoon soy sauce
- 3 shiso leaves
- Steamed Rice
- 1 tablespoon Katsuobushi bonito flakes
- Japanese yellow mustard
- 1 tablespoon green onions
- 1 package Natto

Method:

1. Combine all the components, excluding the shiso and steamed rice.
2. Mix very well until it is dense.
3. Place the rice around and line it with Shiso.

1.9 Vegetable Gyoza

Japanese griddle dumplings are known as gyoza. They began in Asia but have now been adapted to Japanese tastes. The traditional Gyoza stuffing consists of pork and cabbage. When opposed to Chinese dumplings, gyoza has a larger proportion of veggies to meat. You will also note that the dumplings cover is significantly thinner, emphasizing gyoza's crisp feel. Tofu, broccoli, onions, and shiitake mushrooms are filled into these scrumptious Vegetable Gyoza. It is love at first taste with crispy, crunchy bottoms, juicy luscious filling, and handmade dipping sauce! These Asian pan-fried dumplings aren't only for vegetarians or vegans.

Cooking Time: 15 minutes

Serving Size: 2

Ingredients:

Stir Fry

- 3 cups baby spinach
- 14 oz. soft udon noodles
- 1 medium carrot
- 1 cup green onion
- ½ medium onion
- 1 tablespoon vegetable oil

Sauce

- 2 cloves garlic
- 1 teaspoon sesame oil
- 2 tablespoon brown sugar
- 1 tablespoon fresh ginger
- ¼ cup soy sauce
- 2 teaspoon rice wine vinegar
- 2 teaspoon Sambal Oelek

For Garnish

- Additional green onion
- ¼ cup parsley
- Sesame seeds

Method:

1. Put down your veggies after they've been prepared.
2. In a shallow saucepan, combine all of the ingredients to make the sauce.
3. Heat the oil in a large skillet pot or broiler over medium-high heat until it is hot.
4. Cook, occasionally stirring, for about a minute after adding the carrots.
5. Cook, regularly mixing, until vegetables are soft and carrots are ready.
6. Cook for thirty seconds or so, stirring occasionally.
7. Reheat for another thirty seconds, constantly stirring to ensure that everything is well combined.
8. Switch the stir fry to a cup or plate and sprinkle sesame seeds on top.

1.10 Salmon Cucumber Tartare Bites

The prepared salmon tartare nibbles are easy to make and quite tasty. Fresh onions, scallions, lime juice, toasted soy sauce, and fresh cilantro infuse the salmon, making the bites surprisingly spectacular in terms of taste and look. It is a great appetizer for any special occasion and fits into the keto, vegan, low-calorie, and protein diets. That you will never be able to prevent at just one, these bite-sized nibbles are fat-free. Quick and simple to create, these Asian Salmon Cucumber Side dishes are ideal for summer entertainment.

Cooking Time: 50 minutes

Serving Size: 4

Ingredients:

For Serving

- Finely minced scallions
- Black sesame seeds optional
- Japanese seven flavor chili pepper
- 1 English cucumber

Salmon Tartare

- 1 teaspoon mirin
- ½ teaspoon sesame oil
- 2 teaspoons scallions
- 1 teaspoon soy sauce
- ½ pound fresh salmon fillet

Method:

1. Combine the salmon, green onions, sesame oil, mirin, and soy sauce in a medium mixing dish.

2. Cucumber ends should be trimmed.
3. Use a knife; score the cucumber skin laterally.
4. To serve, spoon Salmon Tartare into cucumber circles and marinade with Ichimi Togarashi and white sesame seeds.
5. Serve right away.

1.11 Pancakes Dorayaki

Dorayaki is a traditional Japanese sweet. It comprises two little castella pancake-like burgers folded around a sweet azuki beans puree filling. There was just one layer in the classic Dorayaki. Usagiya in Japan's Ueno area came up with the present design in 1914. Dorayaki is a delicious red bean filling sandwiched between two honey pancakes. In Japan, it is very popular with both children and adults. If you are acquainted with 1970s Japanese cartoons, you are acquainted with this dish thanks to the animated character Doraemon, who is obsessed with them and jumps for any trick surrounding them.

Cooking Time: 20 minutes

Serving Size: 2

Ingredients:

- Vegetable oil
- ½ cup red bean paste
- 2 tablespoon mirin or maple syrup
- ¼ teaspoon soy sauce
- ½ cup sifted cake flour
- 2 teaspoon baking powder
- ⅓ cup soy milk
- 2 tablespoon powdered sugar

Method:

1. In a large cup, mix the flour, icing sugar, and cornstarch.

2. Add the maple syrup, soy milk, and soy sauce to some other dish.

3. To form a delicious mixture, drop the dried mixture into the wet one, and mix.
4. It is not meant to be so dense, but this should be small enough just to pour. For ten minutes, let everything sit.
5. In a non-stick pan or pot, pour that small amount of oil and warm it over moderate flame.
6. To disperse the oil equally, use a towel. You just want the slightest amount to help shade the pancakes but not adhere to them.
7. Reduce heat to medium, and dump about two tablespoons of the batter in as ideal the round as you can find on the non-stick plate.
8. You need all of them to be approximately the same number.
9. For around two minutes, heat on the first hand, bubbles might rise on edge, and the sides will cook very easily.
10. For around one more minute, turn and heat on the other hand.
11. Enable your cakes to chill for several minutes, then add a dollop of Anko, the bean paste, to each of them.
12. To make the Dorayaki, cover it with a croissant and stack it all together.
13. Serve with a swirl of icing sugar or cream cheese or diced strawberries with almond.

1.12 Japanese Ogura Toast

Simply said, Shokupan is buttered Japanese bread with buttery and delicious azuki red peanut sauce on top. It is even nicer with a dollop of fresh cream on top. There aren't a lot of variants on this meal since it is so easy. To make this meal stand out, some people use various toasts, but the appearance is very much the same. Toast, buttered, and red bean jam, with cream on top if desired. When the shokupan is toasted, it offers a beautiful crispy layer on which to apply the butter. The delicious red bean paste is bound together by the creamy butter, which adds "sweetness" to the red bean paste, which is very dry.

Cooking Time: 13 minutes

Serving Size: 8

Ingredients:

- Margarine or butter
- 8 tablespoon whipped cream
- 8 tablespoons red bean paste
- 2 pieces' white bread

Method:

1. Butter the white bread by cutting it into fourths and toasting it until crispy.
2. While the toast is still sweet, spread real cheese or butter on it.
3. On each bread square, spread one tablespoon bean paste powder and one tablespoon cream cheese.

1.13 Vegetable Lo Mein

Lo mein is a traditional wok food that originated in China's food stall scene. Long, supple egg pasta is combined with a savory and tangy sauce, chicken or beef, and many vegetables. The final product is a delightful bowl of slurpy goodness! Lo Mein made with vegetables isn't only for vegetarians. To spice things up, throw in some ground ginger, broccoli, pak choi, green beans, scallops, or even jalapenos. It is a fantastic light lunch or fast meal on a workday. In less than thirty minutes, Veggie Lo Mein delivers excellent meals to your table.

Cooking Time: 25 minutes

Serving Size: 4

Ingredients:

- ½ cup snow peas
- 3 cups baby spinach
- 1 red bell pepper
- 1 carrot
- 8 ounces egg noodles
- 2 cloves garlic
- 2 cups cremini mushrooms
- 1 tablespoon olive oil

For the Sauce

- ½ teaspoon ground ginger
- ½ teaspoon Sriracha
- 2 teaspoons sugar

- 1 teaspoon sesame oil
- 2 tablespoons soy sauce

Method:
1. Set down a bowl full containing sesame oil, sugar, soy sauce, spice, and Sriracha.
2. Heat pasta as per package directions in a large pot of water; rinse well.
3. In a medium saucepan or skillet, heat the olive oil over medium heat.
4. Garlic, onions, red pepper, and carrot are added to the pan.
5. Mix in the green beans and spinach for around 2-3 minutes, or until the kale ripens.
6. Toss in the egg noodles with the soy sauce combination and toss gently to blend.
7. Serve right away.

Chapter 2: Vegetarian Japanese Lunch and Dinner Recipes

2.1 Vegetarian Ramen

This ramen base is very creamy and thick, and it can fool you into believing it is Tonkotsu. In Japanese, soy milk noodles are not always vegan or vegetarian. The broth may be produced using pig bone or poultry carcass, like ordinary Tonkotsu, Eel sauce, or Miso soup. Most ramen soups include a seafood-based broth made with bonito particles and kelp to add to the soup's complexity. Use dashi, powdered shiitake mushrooms, and wakame to make this recipe vegan and vegetarian.

Cooking Time: 1 hour

Serving Size: 4

> **Ingredients:**
> - 4 baby bok choy
> - 4 5-oz. packages ramen noodles
> - 3 tablespoons unsalted butter
> - 1 tablespoon soy sauce
> - 4 garlic cloves
> - 8 dried shiitake mushrooms
> - 1 piece dried kombu
> - ¼ cup vegetable oil
> - 1 2" piece ginger
> - 2 tablespoon tomato paste
> - 1 tablespoon black sesame seeds
> - Kosher salt

- 4 scallions
- 1 tablespoon gochugaru

Method:

1. Cook the garlic and ¼ cup of the oil in a medium saucepan over medium heat, frequently whisking, until the garlic is translucent, around four minutes.
2. Heat the remaining two tablespoons of oil to moderate in the preserved pot.
3. Insert the tomato sauce and simmer for about two minutes, stirring regularly, before it appears to adhere to the sides of the pan and blackens gradually.
4. Insert the Kombu and mushroom, then whisk in five cups of cold water.
5. Move the solids to a mixer using a rubber spatula.
6. To mix, add a spoonful or two of liquid and purée until creamy.
7. Add oil a slice at a time, until introducing more, whisking to mix with each addition.
8. In the meantime, put it to a boil with a big pot of water. Insert bok choy and cook for about two minutes until it is greenish and soft.

2.2 Japanese Mitarashi Dango

Rice dumplings impaled on stalks in groups of 3–5 and glazed with a rich soy sauce glaze are known as mitarashi Dango. Mitarashi Dango was created in Kyoto's Kamo Mitarashi Tea Garden. The Dango was considered to be prepared as a sacrifice to the deities, and the term was derived from the mitarashi of a well-known temple in the city. Dango was first sold as a snack by street sellers in Kyoto, and it quickly became famous among tourists. Mitarashi Dango is now available in supermarkets, corner shops, and specialized sweet shops all around Japan. Its crystalline coating and charred scent distinguish it.

Cooking Time: 15 minutes

Serving Size: 2

Ingredients:
- 4 tablespoon filtered water
- ½ cup sweet rice flour (mochiko)

Sauce
- 2 teaspoon mirin
- 1 teaspoon arrowroot starch
- 1 tablespoon soy sauce
- 1 tablespoon coconut sugar
- 3 tablespoon filtered water

Other
- Wood skewers
- Toasted nori sheet

Method:
1. Over moderate flame, ready a pot of boiling water, and bring it to a boil when cooking your Dango flour.
2. Mix the water and sweet rice flour in a measuring dish.
3. Proceed with a spoon and mix to blend, then begin using your hands to work the flour.
4. Break into 6 bits and shape into little balls until you have a functional dough.
5. Drop softly into the pot while the water boils and steam for about five minutes, and until the Dango is floating and is baked all the time through.
6. First, mix gluten-free soy sauce, coconut sugar, water, and mirin in a shallow skillet over medium heat.
7. Stir to mix, add the slurry of arrowroot flour and begin stirring until the mixture thickens.
8. Turn off the heat until the sauce thickens, then put it aside.
9. Drain the Dango again, though, and skewer three bits with each piece.
10. Glaze to the palate of your sweet soy glaze and eat!

2.3 Vegetarian Okonomiyaki

Okonomiyaki is a savory Japanese pancake made with wheat flour and various fillings; it is an illustration of konamono. The name comes from the Japanese words okonomi, which means "what you like" or "whatever you prefer," and yaki, which means "prepared." This veggie okonomiyaki is a simplified version of classic Japanese cuisine, consisting of beautiful tiny cabbage patties that are considerably sweeter than they should be. The greatest results are achieved when the cabbage is shredded very thinly. If your cauliflower is too rough, it won't stay together as well, and the consistency will be thicker and less elegant. This veggie okonomiyaki with yolks, lettuce, pak choi, and red onion will boost your diet. It is a low-calorie, nutritious lunch alternative.

Cooking Time: 30 minutes

Serving Size: 2

Ingredients:

- 2 spring onions, thinly sliced
- 1 tablespoon oil
- 120 grams shredded green cabbage
- 1 small carrot, grated
- ½ teaspoon pureed ginger
- Black pepper
- 4 eggs
- 1 tablespoon soy sauce
- 80 grams plain flour

To Serve

- Chopped spring onions

- Sesame seeds
- Sriracha
- Mayonnaise or salad cream

Method:
1. In a blending pan, beat the eggs and then insert the flour.
2. Mix to shape the mixture for the pancake.
3. Include the pureed ginger and soy sauce, lots of black pepper, then insert the carrot, cabbage, and spring onions that are finely chopped.
4. Heat for several minutes over medium-high heat.
5. Repeat to make four pancakes in sum with the leftover pancake combination.

2.4 Japanese Soba Noodles

Soba is a buckwheat-based thin Japanese pasta. Buckwheat noodles, often known as soba in Japanese, are richer in protein and fiber than most other pasta. They contain therapeutic properties, as do many Japanese products, and have been demonstrated to help manage blood sugar, enhance heart health, relieve symptoms, and perhaps prevent cancer. The noodles may be eaten cold with a side dish or heated in a noodle soup. Wheat flour is used in the Nagano soba type. Soba noodles are simple to come by and don't need a trip to a specialist or Asian grocery shop. Soba noodles may be found in various venues in Japan, ranging from junk food to high-end specialized restaurants.

Cooking Time: 20 minutes

Serving Size: 6

Ingredients:

- ½ cup green onions minced
- 3 tablespoons sesame seeds
- 1 tablespoon canola oil
- 2 cups green onions
- 10 ounces Soba Buckwheat Noodles
- ¼ teaspoon ground black pepper
- 1 tablespoon sugar
- 1/3 cup Double Fermented Soy Sauce
- 3 tablespoons toasted sesame oil
- 2 tablespoons rice vinegar

Method:
1. Carry a big pot of water on the stove and make soup the soba pasta for five minutes or even just until soft, occasionally mixing so the pasta does not tangle.
2. Wash in a colander and pat dry under ice water, dumping to erase the starch.
3. When the pasta is frying, sweep the sesame oil, soy sauce, sugar rice vinegar, and black pepper together in such a small dish. And put aside.
4. Over medium flame, heat a large skillet.
5. Insert the canola oil and flame the sliced spring onions until they glitter.
6. Heat for fifteen seconds or until aromatic, mixing.
7. Insert the sesame and soy mixture and reheat for thirty seconds.
8. Put the pasta and toss till the pasta is warmed through.
9. Insert the leftover minced spring onions and a quarter of the seeds.
10. Garnish with the residual seeds and eat at low temperatures or hotter.

2.5 Soy-Glazed Eggplant Donburi

It is a thinly chopped eggplant cooked till lightly browned and served over a steaming dish of rice with sweet soy sauce. This Plant-based Eggplant Donburi is a Traditional vegan rice dish that deserves recognition at your plate on a weeknight. The standout element in this rice dish, without question, is the eggplant. Consider it the cheese of the vegetable kingdom. It is light and adaptable, allowing it to take on practically any taste. The structural integrity of eggplant and its velvety, meaty, and exquisite feel distinguishes it from other vegetables. The greatest, richest flavor comes from grilling the eggplant until it is well browned. It also produces a soft buttery feel with a crunchy edge that is difficult to resist.

Cooking Time: 20 minutes

Serving Size: 2

Ingredients:

- 4 tablespoons neutral-flavored oil
- ½ teaspoon white sesame seeds
- 1 knob ginger
- 2 tablespoon potato starch
- 10 shiso leaves
- 7 oz. Japanese eggplant

Seasonings

- 2 tablespoon soy sauce
- 4 tablespoon mirin

Method:

1. Collect all the components.

2. Round the eggplant into ¼-inch pieces and insert iodine.
3. Put aside for fifteen minutes and put a hand towel to clean off the humidity.
4. Wash the shiso leaf and use a hand towel to clear. Dispose of the ends.
5. Heat 2 tablespoons of oil over medium-high heat in a cooking pot.
6. Add the eggplant pieces to a thin layer when the pan is heated.
7. Cook till it is nicely browned on the back end, around three minutes.
8. Do not hit the eggplants before then to obtain a good sear.
9. Whenever the lowest surface is perfectly fried, sprinkle on top of the remaining oil (2 tablespoons) and turn the eggplant slices for around 3-4 minutes to fry the other half.
10. Take it down to a boil and spill the sauce a couple of times over the eggplant.
11. Spray with seeds and decorate with shiso leaves. Instantly serve.

2.6 Spicy Tofu Bento Bowl

This salad adds an Asian twist to traditional vegetable elements. Bento relates to bento boxes, which are compartmentalized containers used in Japan for take-along meals. A dried basil and soy sauce is used to flavor and sear the hot tofu. The concoction is served on a mound of white rice, baby spinach, chopped carrots, chopped cucumbers, and velvety avocado. The final touch is a dusting of toasted sesame seeds, which adds an oriental flavor to this salad. There's marinated tofu, toasted hazelnut furikake on grains, and many veggies in this vegan bento box. This colorful vegetarian bento box is a great lunch idea with lots of vegetables, and it is easy to prepare ahead of time.

Cooking Time: 30 minutes

Serving Size: 6

Ingredients:

- 2 tablespoon sesame seeds
- 2-3 scallions, sliced thinly
- 1 teaspoon red chili flakes
- 1 lb. broccolini, about 12 stalks
- 2 garlic cloves, finely minced
- 2 teaspoon ginger, minced
- 1 tablespoon white miso paste
- 1 tablespoon brown sugar
- 1 cup dry brown or white rice
- 3 tablespoon soy sauce
- 2 tablespoon rice vinegar
- 3 tablespoon sesame oil

- 6 Portobello mushrooms

Method:
1. In a cup, combine the sesame oil, chili-garlic sauce, and soy sauce.
2. Over medium-high heat, warm a pan. Soak the tofu in a soy sauce combination; boil for ten minutes, or until golden brown.
3. Transfer the leftover chili combination to the spring onions, cream, and lime juice. Toss on the tofu.
4. In a cup, combine the soy sauce, lime juice, spice, and chili-garlic sauce.
5. Add rice in bowls for dining. Top of the Greens.
6. Trim carrot stripes with a cheese grater over the end.
7. Place the tofu, celery, and carrot on top. Slather with sesame seeds; eat with a combination of soya sauce.

2.7 Japanese Rice Balls with Avocado Filling and Sweet Potato

In Japan, onigiri (filled rice balls) are a staple diet. Onigiri is usually eaten cold, but this yaki (which means "fried") is best eaten shortly after they've been cooked. Yaki onigiri is made crispy by quickly frying them in a hot skillet. When coated in a homemade teriyaki sauce, these butternut squash and avocado yaki onigiri become even more delicious. This tiny nibble was made much more delectable by the sweet and salty sauce. Onigiri is a wonderful party finger meal, especially for road trips or vacations. If you have ever wanted to create sushi but didn't want to deal with all the slicing and rolling, onigiri is a great alternative.

Cooking Time: 1 hour

Serving Size: 4

Ingredients:
- 1 teaspoon toasted sesame oil
- ½ avocado
- ½ teaspoon salt
- ½ – 1 small sweet potato
- 2 tablespoon rice wine vinegar
- 1 tablespoon sugar
- 3 cups water
- ¼ cup sesame seeds
- 1 ½ cup brown sushi rice

Teriyaki Sauce
- 2 tablespoons sugar
- 1 tablespoon rice wine vinegar

- 5 tablespoons soy sauce
- 5 tablespoons mirin
- Vegetable oil for frying

Method:
1. Begin by doing the rice cleaning.
2. Use ice water to coat the rice, put the pot on the flame, and protect it with a cover. Switch the heat off when the water heats.
3. Offer it a stirring and allow the water to consume the rice.
4. Strip a large mixing bowl with films from the kitchen and drop around one tablespoon of cooled rice in it.
5. With certain rice, surround the stuffing and push it into a standardized ball.
6. Continue cooking until you have caramelized the sauce. Switch the heat off over the pan.

2.8 Lightly Fried Japanese Vegetables

Teppanyaki is a traditional Japanese dish made up of lightly cooked veggies that are typically eaten with rice. Julienned courgette, onions, and white lettuce are used in this version of the meal. Vegetable teppanyaki is a teppanyaki dish that consists of a variety of foods cooked in a teppan. Green beans, broccoli, mushrooms, peas, courgettes, peppers, and carrots are examples of these veggies. The veggies are sautéed in a pan with a zesty, delicate sauce and may be served alone or with your favorite grain. Veggie teppanyaki is comparatively simple to make, with the only difficult part being readying the veggies. They must be cut properly so that they finish cooking. □

Cooking Time: 20 minutes

Serving Size: 2

Ingredients:

- Sea salt
- Toasted sesame seeds
- ¼ white cabbage, julienned
- 2 teaspoons mirin
- Sesame oil
- 1 tablespoon rice wine vinegar
- 1 tablespoon tamari
- 2 carrots, julienned
- 1 small red bell pepper
- 1 small white onion
- 4 spring onions, chopped
- 1 zucchini, thinly sliced

Method:
1. Over a high flame, warm up a big wok.
2. Insert the sesame oil and transfer the veggies until it is close to the combustion mark.
3. Let them stay in a wok until half of the wok is dark on one edge.
4. Mix the tamari, vinegar, and mirin of rice wine.
5. When stirring, spray the combination over the veggies to offer them some humidity.
6. To ensure they are always crisp, cook the veggies for two minutes.
7. If required, sprinkle them with kosher salt, put them on serving plates, and marinade them with toasted pine nuts.

2.9 Tofu Yasai Don

It takes some cutting to make this donburi (Japan rice bowl), but once you have done that, it comes around each other rapidly and effortlessly. Tofu, parsley roots, Shallots, Japan butternut squash, and other ingredients are cooked in a sweet, savory sauce before being served over a mound of rice. Simple but delectable! Just be sure to start preparing the tofu three days ahead of time, so it is ready when you need it. This Stir Fry Vegetable dish allows you to prepare a nutritious supper for your family on a hectic weekday. It is packed with veggies and your choice of proteins, and it takes less than thirty minutes to prepare.

Cooking Time: 2 hours

Serving Size: 4

> **Ingredients:**
> - 4 green onions, sliced
> - 4 teaspoons white sesame seeds
> - 3 rehydrated Shiitake mushrooms
> - 6-8 cups steamed Japanese rice
> - 2/3 cup mirin
> - 1 tablespoon fresh ginger juice
> - 1 14-ounce block extra firm tofu
> - 2 cups kombu Shiitake dashi
> - 2/3 cup reduced-sodium tamari
> - 4 ounces frozen, shelled edamame
> - 2 slender carrots, peeled
> - 1 medium Japanese sweet potato
> - 1 slender burdock root

Method:
1. Wash the tofu and wipe it off with a hand towel.
2. Cover in a plastic wrap sheet and afterward cover in an aluminum sheet.
3. Refrigerate in the fridge for 24 hours. In the oven, melt.
4. Do not unpack tofu, but put it in a jar, sealed, as the liquid can leak.
5. It can take one to two nights to melt.
6. Once the tofu has thawed full, unscrew it and rinse off the excess moisture, then put it on a serving platter filled with many sheets of clean cloth.
7. Put on top some more sheets of the towel and then place it on the edge of a work surface.
8. With something like many food containers or a magazine, load the chopping board back and then let the tofu push for at least thirty minutes.
9. Break it into thin pieces until the tofu has been pounded, then put it aside.
10. Unpack it and brush off the excess moisture until the tofu has defrosted entirely, then put it on a serving platter filled with many sheets of clean cloth.
11. Put on top some more sheets of the towel, then place on each of that a work surface.
12. Use anything like multiple boxes of beans or a notebook to force the work surface back and let the tofu push for at least thirty minutes.
13. Break it into thin pieces until the tofu has been pounded, then put it aside.
14. Place the edamame, chilled and camped, in a jar and fill it with liquid. Over moderate flame,

carry the mixture to a boil, then extract the water and drain. Place back the defrosted edamame.

15. Use the end of a paring knife, scrape off from the outside coating of the burdock core, and slice it.

16. Begin at the heavier side and slice it lengthwise, with the blade at a 45° angle, about half-inch from the bottom.

17. Push the burdock core to you, flip approximately 1/3, and cut once more, helping to keep the knife figuring at the same 45 ° F viewpoint.

18. Continue to cut that way, varying your cuts' width and angles if required to create tiny pieces. Use the same tool, cut the sliced vegetables.

19. Lengthwise, split the stripped Japanese zucchini in the quarter, then lengthwise, split each quarter in the quarter again.

20. Break each quarter lengthways into ½-inch thinly sliced.

21. In a small saucepan, mix the dashi, mirin, low sodium tamari, and spice extract. Brought to a gentle simmer over medium-high heat.

22. Insert the burdock root, Japanese sweet potato, tofu, carrots, and mushroom bits and boil until all the veggies are soft, uncovered.

23. To sustain a steady simmer while you steam the veggies, reduce heat as required.

24. Insert the edamame and bake for an extra minute, enabling the frying pan to heat it and consume the flavors.

25. Place 1 and a half cups of warm rice into personal donburi baskets or big, shallow broth bowls to fit the rice bowls.

26. The vegetables and tofu represent the rice. Spoon over each cup with a few teaspoons of frying liquid.

27. Marinade and serve instantly with finely diced spring onion and toasted pumpkin seeds.

2.10 Yasai Itame

"Yasai" signifies veggies in Japanese, while "itame" is the adjective form of the verb "itameru," which indicates "to stir fry." Although the name suggests that Yasai Itame is a vegetarian meal, it generally incorporates a tiny quantity of finely diced meat or sausages. Yasai Itame is a popular home cooking meal that has been around for a long time. It combines veggies and meat in a single meal. And not just a single kind of food, but a variety of brightly colored veggies. Don't be overly concerned about what goes nicely together. Stir-fry meals are ideal for using little bits and pieces of food that have been stored in the refrigerator. This is a simple Japanese recipe that doesn't call for any special ingredients. This is a fresh variety you may rely on whether you are new to cooking or don't cook very frequently.

Cooking Time: 30 minutes

Serving Size: 4

Ingredients:

- 1 tablespoon neutral-flavored oil
- 3.5 oz. bean sprouts
- 1 clove garlic
- 1 knob ginger
- 6.5 oz. thinly sliced pork
- ¼ cabbage

- ½ carrot
- ¼ onion
- 10 snow peas

For Pork Marinade

- 1 teaspoon sake
- 1 teaspoon soy sauce

For Seasonings

- Freshly ground black pepper
- 2 teaspoon sesame oil
- 1 teaspoon soy sauce
- ½ teaspoon kosher salt
- 1 teaspoon oyster sauce

Method:

1. Assemble all the components.
2. If needed, cut meat into tiny chunks and sauté the beef in a shallow saucepan with one teaspoon of soy sauce and one teaspoon of sake.
3. Strip the snow peas from the loops and cut the onions into small strips.
4. Heat 2 tablespoons of olive oil over moderate heat in a large deep fryer or skillet.
5. Insert the onion and cook till almost soft, then add the carrots and mix.
6. Insert the broccoli and green beans as the carrot is growing soft.
7. Keep stirring the components and mix.
8. Insert one tablespoon of oyster sauce and one teaspoon of soya sauce.

9. Insert the cinnamon, chili flakes, freshly roasted, and drizzle with two teaspoons of sesame oil.

2.11 Cucumber Sunomono

Sunomono is vinegar-based meals that are often offered as a green salad to the main meal. Su is a Japanese word that meaning vinegar. The sourness of the acid helps in stimulating your appetite, so these mild, crisp sour greens are a fantastic start to any dinner. These cucumber salads make a fantastic seasonal side dish, particularly grilled meat or fish, when our bodies tend to 'refrigerate' foods. Aside from being simple to make, the salad is tangy and crispy, and the health advantages are incentive enough to eat it regularly. This sweet and savory cucumber salad is cooked in vinegar, honey, salt, and sesame oil and makes a great side dish. It is light, nutritious, and quite hydrating. This is one of the most common appetizers served at Japanese dinner tables, and that it is quick and easy to make.

Cooking Time: 1 hour 15 minutes

Serving Size: 5

Ingredients:
- 1 teaspoon salt
- 1 ½ teaspoons ginger root
- ⅓ cup rice vinegar
- 4 teaspoons white sugar
- 2 large cucumbers, peeled

Method:
1. Cucumbers should be split in half lengthwise, and any big seeds should be scooped out.
2. Cut into very small pieces crosswise.

3. Combine the vinegar, starch, salt, and seasoning in a shallow cup. Mix well.
4. Put cucumbers in the cup and swirl to cover them with the solution evenly.
5. Before eating, chill the cucumber dish for at least 1 hour.

2.12 Mashed Tofu Salad with Green Bean

Shiraae, also known as smashed tofu salad, is a traditional Japanese meal prepared with soft green beans, velvety tofu, crunchy sesame seeds, and savory miso. This vegetarian salad comes up quickly and maybe served at your dinner table. You can always find a colorful range of veggie salads in Japanese household cuisine, ranging from collard greens to western-style side salad to steamed veggies. They provide a whole meal flavor and nutrition. Green beans and chard are boiled and flavored with soy sauce before mixed in with the tofu combination. The tofu supplies all of the nutrition, while the greens give color, structure, and freshness. As a result, this recipe is vegan-friendly and suitable for anyone.

Cooking Time: 30 minutes

Serving Size: 2

Ingredients:
- 9 oz. green beans
- 7 oz. silken tofu

Seasonings
- 1 teaspoon soy sauce
- ⅛ teaspoon kosher salt
- 1 tablespoon sugar
- 2 teaspoon miso
- 4 tablespoon white sesame seeds

Method:
1. Collect all the products.
2. On a sheet or pan, place the sealed tofu.

3. On top of the tofu, place another plate or tray and carry a massive item on top to allow drainage. Place thirty minutes free.
4. Put to a boil a huge pot of boiling water.
5. Boil up the crisp-tender green beans.
6. Well, rinse and put aside.
7. Break the green beans into small bits horizontally.
8. Pour in the soy sauce and mix them around. For later, put aside.
9. In a cooking pot, roast the sesame seeds, constantly tossing the wok.
10. Use the hands to split it into bits and transfer it to the sesame seed combination.
11. Tasting the tofu and seasoning with salts to taste is essential.
12. When mixed, you can cool for thirty minutes in the fridge before eating or serve instantly.

2.13 Japanese Rice Balls with Avocado Filling

Sushi rice may be used for a variety of purposes. Making Onigiri, or Japanese-packed rice balls is yet another fun way to utilize it. Since these rice balls are simple to create and completely customizable, onigiri is great food in Japan. Sushi rice is usually mildly salted, but you may use black, brownish, or red rice alternatively if you want to be more daring. Mix the contents and rice so that each mouthful contains something tasty, but the conventional method merely fills the balls. Cover your rice balls with seaweed, finely chopped avocado, dried basil, or sesame seeds as a final step.

Cooking Time: 1 hour

Serving Size: 4

Ingredients:

- 1 teaspoon toasted sesame oil
- ½ avocado
- ½ teaspoon salt
- ½ – 1 small sweet potato
- 2 tablespoon rice wine vinegar
- 1 tablespoon sugar
- 3 cups water
- ¼ cup sesame seeds
- 1 ½ cup brown sushi rice

Teriyaki Sauce

- 2 tablespoons sugar
- 1 tablespoon rice wine vinegar

- 5 tablespoons soy sauce
- 5 tablespoons mirin
- Vegetable oil for frying

Method:
1. Begin by doing the rice cleaning.
2. Use ice water to coat the rice, put the pot on the flame, and protect it with a cover. Switch the heat off when the water heats.
3. Offer it a stirring and allow the water to consume the rice.
4. Strip a large mixing bowl with films from the kitchen and drop around one tablespoon of cooled rice in it.
5. With certain rice, surround the stuffing and push it into a standardized ball.
6. Continue cooking until you have caramelized the sauce. Switch the heat off over the pan.

2.14 Yakitori Grilled Skewers

These Japanese poultry and vegetable kebabs are difficult to resist, coated in a handmade Yakitori sauce. You will like this easy Yakitori dish with buttery flavor sauce! It is perfect for outside grilling or broiling. When it comes to poultry on a stick, they have their variation called Yakitori in Japan. Yakitori means "grilled chicken," but it also represents good times and joyful hours in Japan. Chicken skewers are a traditional dish offered at an izakaya, Japanese-tapas-style taverns where icy beer, delectable nibbles, and merry banter are all part of the experience. They are also the kind of classic dish you will find at specialty restaurants that specialize in Yakitori.

Cooking Time: 1 hour 5 minutes

Serving Size: 1

Ingredients:

- Spring onions
- Chicken breast

Suggested Additional Items

- Asparagus
- Firm tofu
- Pork belly slices
- Green pepper
- Leek

Sauce

- 1-2 teaspoon katakuriko potato starch
- Shichimi pepper seasoning
- 3 tablespoon soy sauce

- 2 tablespoon sugar
- 1 tablespoon mirin
- 1 tablespoon cooking sake

Method:
1. In a bowl with two sugar tables, combine the boiling sake, miso, and sesame oil.
2. In a small saucepan, mix a little katakuriko rice flour in water and heat the mixture while boiling it.
3. Start glazing the slicer components with your yakitori sauces using a baking brush.
4. Begin by setting the skewers on the grill in an environment where the heat is high and even.
5. Switch the yakitori often to ensure even cooking, and sprinkle more yakitori sauces onto the meat each time.
6. The meat will be edible once it has turned golden brown.

2.15 Vegetable Yakisoba

Yakisoba is a traditional Japanese meat and vegetables stir-fry pasta dish flavored with a sweet and salty sauce comparable to Worcestershire sauce. Yakisoba, or Japanese stir-fried noodles, first appeared in the 1930s as So-su (Soup) Yakisoba, and by the late 1950s, it had become a popular child's snack at mom-and-pop confectionery shops. Yakisoba has been made and eaten at homes and Teishoku-ya (Japanese restaurants) since then and has become a symbol of Japanese street cuisine. Yakisoba food stands are common at school events, celebrations, and snack stores since it is simple to set up a metal plate Teppan and obtain ingredients to produce this cuisine. Yakisoba is a simple dish to prepare, and you can customize it by adding practically any components. For Meatless Monday, try it with fish or a simple vegan version.

Cooking Time: 40 minutes

Serving Size: 10

Ingredients:

- 16 oz. yakisoba noodles
- 3 tablespoon oil
- ¼ small cabbage
- 1 large onion
- ½ lb. broccoli
- 2 large carrots
- 1 large sweet bell pepper

Yakisoba Sauce

- 2 tablespoon ketchup
- 4 tablespoon Worcestershire sauce

- 2 tablespoon soy sauce
- 2 tablespoon oyster sauce
- 2 tablespoon sugar

Method:
1. Mix all yakisoba liquid ingredients in a large bowl and set aside.
2. Heat a small amount of oil in a skillet over high heat.
3. Return all of the veggies to the same pan. Separate the noodles as directed on the box. Toss in the noodles in the skillet.
4. Toss all together after pouring the sauce over the components.
5. Reduce the heat to medium-low and cook for five minutes.
6. Take it off the heat and enjoy it!

2.16 Japanese Fruit Sandwich

Fruit Sando, a Traditional fruit snack, will improve your morning! Between two pieces of pillow Japanese dairy bread, juicy, seasonally fresh fruits are immersed in cooled whipped cream. These bright strawberry, lemon, and kiwi toast are great for breakfast or supper. It is a shokupan burger with vegetables and fruits and creamy sandwiched between two pieces of Japanese dairy bread. While the bread is puffy and pillow, the filling is the star of the show. The sandwich's centerpiece is an asymmetrically designed strawberry, orange, kiwi, mango, and blueberry sandwich. The silky and buttery whipped cream between the bread and strawberries adds a dreamlike element to the dish. It is bright, fresh, and tastes like sunshine in a sandwich.

Cooking Time: 10 minutes

Serving Size: 4

Ingredients:

- ¼ teaspoon vanilla extract
- 8 slices Japanese sandwich bread
- ½ pint heavy cream
- 3½ tablespoons milk
- 1 mango
- 14 strawberries
- 1 kiwi fruit

Method:

1. Cut the kiwifruit into ¾-inch thick circles after peeling and slicing it.

2. Remove the peel from the mango, remove the tapered ends, and cut it into ¾-inch wide batons.
3. Strawberry tops can be removed. If they are too big, cut them in half.
4. In a cold pan, whisk together the heavy cream, condensed milk, and vanilla essence until strong peaks emerge.
5. Fruit should be put on top of the whipped cream.
6. Take the crusts from the four remaining bits of toast and cover the sandwiches.
7. Cut them in half or quarters until you are about to eat them.

Chapter 3: Vegetarian Japanese Snack, Soups, and Salad Recipes

3.1 Miso Soup with Tofu, Wakame Seaweed

Making real Japanese miso soup at household is simple! Homemade miso soup, the everyday medicine of the Japanese diet, is tasty and has several health advantages. Most Japanese dinners come with a bowl of boiled vegetables and a bowl of Miso Soup, a classic Japanese soup. Many different types of miso soup are consumed in Japan, depending on the location, weather, and personal taste. We create the soup using a variety of ingredients in comparison to the original tofu and wakame combo. As a result, we never grow tired of it. Miso soup consists of three ingredients: dashi, miso (soybean paste), and any ingredients you like.

Cooking Time: 15 minutes

Serving Size: 2

Ingredients:

- ½ cup chopped green onion
- ¼ cup firm tofu
- 3-4 tablespoon yellow miso paste
- ½ cup chopped green chard
- 1 sheet nori
- 4 cups vegetable broth

Method:

1. In a small mixing bowl, put the vegetable broth and take it to a low boil.
2. Meanwhile, place the miso in a shallow saucepan, add a little warmer water, and swirl until soft.

3. When transferred to the broth later, this would guarantee that it does not clump. Just put it aside.
4. Transfer chard, spring onions, and tofu to the liquid and cook for five minutes.
5. Insert nori, next, and mix. Add the miso solution, detach from the flame, and whisk to blend.
6. When desired, try and add additional miso or a touch of kosher salt.
7. Serve it warm. It is better when clean.

3.2 Creamy Miso Pasta with Tofu and Asparagus

This Delicious Miso Pasta with Paneer and Asparagus is the perfect springtime comfort dish! It is filling and bursting with flavor. It is the tastiest plant-based supper you will ever have in under 20 minutes. Tofu is a good source of plant-based protein, while asparagus is high in minerals and fiber. It is soy milk, not heavy cream or ordinary milk! Soy milk is a hidden ingredient in Japanese cuisine to provide sweetness and smoothness to meals such as vegetarian noodle broth, fried rice, and pasta. It is a plant-based and delicious addition to vegetarian or vegan dishes. Cream basis, tomato basis, Japanese-style dashi foundation, seafood stock foundation, vegetable broth foundation, and so on are some of the Soup Pasta varieties. Consider it pasta with a modest quantity of flavorful broth. Soup pasta is traditionally served with a fork and a spoon. Soup and pasta have such a great world to offer!

Cooking Time: 20 minutes

Serving Size: 2

Ingredients:

For Pasta

- ¼ teaspoon kosher
- Freshly ground black pepper
- 1 firm fried tofu
- 1 tablespoon olive oil
- 4 oz. asparagus

For Cooking Spaghetti

- 2 teaspoon miso
- 1 teaspoon soy sauce
- Soy milk sauce
- ½ cup unsweetened soy milk
- 7 oz. spaghetti
- 1 ½ tablespoon sea salt

Method:
1. Collect all the components.
2. Mix a half cup of soy milk, two teaspoons of miso, and one teaspoon of soy sauce in a mixing cup and blend it.
3. Approximately twice the sum of these components if you want to turn it into "soup noodles."
4. With a clean cloth, cover the tofu and extract any humidity. Split into small pieces of tofu.
5. Cut off the asparagus edges and cut them into small slices horizontally.
6. Begin to boil four quarters of water in a big saucepan. Put one and a half tablespoons of salt and pasta until boiling.
7. To the bowl, transfer the soy flour mixture and reduce the heat to a moderate flame.
8. For separate pots, serve the spaghetti.

3.3 Green Bean Shiraae (Mashed Tofu Salad with Green Bean)

Shiraae, also known as smashed tofu salad, is a traditional Japanese meal prepared with soft green beans, velvety tofu, crunchy sesame seeds, and savory miso. This vegetarian salad comes up quickly and maybe served at your dinner table. You can always find a colorful range of veggie salads in Japanese household cuisine, ranging from collard greens to western-style side salad to steamed veggies. They provide a whole meal flavor and nutrition. Green beans and chard are boiled and flavored with soy sauce before mixed in with the tofu combination. The tofu supplies all of the nutrition, while the greens give color, structure, and freshness. As a result, this recipe is vegan-friendly and suitable for anyone.

Cooking Time: 30 minutes

Serving Size: 2

Ingredients:

- 9 oz. green beans
- 7 oz. silken tofu

Seasonings

- 1 teaspoon soy sauce
- ⅛ teaspoon kosher salt
- 1 tablespoon sugar
- 2 teaspoon miso
- 4 tablespoon white sesame seeds

Method:

1. Collect all the products.

2. Hold it in an enclosed jar and add water before it fills the tofu to hold the remaining tofu.
3. Leave it in the fridge (start changing the water daily) and use it for a few periods.
4. You would not want to drain water from the tofu fully, but some humidity must be removed so that the coating does not become too wet.
5. Place paper towels around the tofu.
6. On a sheet or pan, place the sealed tofu.
7. On top of the tofu, place another plate or tray and carry a massive item on top to allow drainage. Place thirty minutes free.
8. Put to a boil a huge pot of boiling water. Blow the sides of the green beans apart.
9. Boil up the crisp-tender green beans.
10. Well, rinse and put aside.
11. Break the green beans into small bits horizontally.
12. Pour in the soy sauce and mix them around. For later, put aside.
13. In a cooking pot, roast the sesame seeds, constantly tossing the wok, till they are aromatic and starting to pop. Switch to a Japanese mortar.
14. With a pestle, crush seeds.
15. Add the miso and honey.
16. Mix well before the crushed sesame seeds are mixed into the sugars and miso.
17. Withdraw the tofu from the clean cloth.
18. Use the hands to split it into bits and transfer it to the sesame seed combination.
19. Tasting the tofu and seasoning with salts to taste is essential. It is not meant to be dull.

20. Put all together till perfect.
21. Be careful to first clean off some surplus soy sauce from the beans.
22. Just the seasoning will weaken the fluid from the soy sauce.
23. The cooked green beans are then added to the tofu seasoning. Mix well.
24. When mixed, you can cool for thirty minutes in the fridge before eating or serve instantly.

3.4 Tofu Katsu with Spicy Sweet-Sour Sauce

This variation of katsu, a Japanese-style cooked fillet dish, is made a little healthier by using tofu slabs. The slabs are dipped in spiced bread crumbs, baked rather than deep-fried, and served with quinoa for a complete, protein-rich meal. It is also worth noting that the remaining katsu reheats well: Simply bake it for ten minutes at 400 degrees in the oven. They are crunchy and tempting, particularly when dipped in a bowl of sweet and sour sauce. You may eat them with a cool beer, scatter them over a stir-fry, or pack them into a bánh mi sandwich by cutting tofu into segments rather than cubes.

Cooking Time: 15 minutes

Serving Size: 24

Ingredients:

- Sunflower or canola oil
- Sweet chili sauce, to serve
- ½ cup Aquafaba
- ½-1 cup breadcrumbs
- 200 grams' firm tofu

- 2 tablespoons plain flour
- Soy sauce

Method:
1. First, to eliminate the extra humidity and digest flavors faster, we have to 'push' the tofu.
2. Shift it to a fresh one until the paper towel gets wet. Repeat till the hand towel remains almost clean.
3. When the tofu is pounded, split the cube in half and finish with two layers that are fifty percent thinner.
4. Pour ample soy sauce so that the tofu is at least half immersed.
5. Left it for thirty minutes to marinate, then turn over the tofu bits and keep for the next 30 minutes in soy sauce.
6. To create an even coverage on both sides, ensure you push each square's surface into the powder and cornflour well.
7. Push few more bits of tofu into the butter.

3.5 Vegetarian Katsu Curry

This vegetarian soy katsu curry will satisfy all of your takeout cravings while still leaving you craving more! The onion, clove, carrot, and ginger in this katsu curry sauce are fried first. The seasonings, mirin (sweet Japanese wine), chopped tomatoes, soy sauce, and veggie stock are added. If you can't get exceptionally hard tofu, use a tofu press to push out as much water as possible. Additionally, seitan, which has a meatier texture, might be used. Serve with panko-breaded tofu in a velvety carrot curry sauce.

Cooking Time: 15 minutes

Serving Size: 2

Ingredients:

- 1 cup frozen stir fry vegetables
- Cooked rice
- 2 vegetarian schnitzels
- 1 block of Golden Curry

Method:

1. As advised, prepare the schnitzels or cutlets.
2. Break and set it aside into pieces.
3. Steam a pan and cook the veggies that are frozen.
4. To loosen the curry cube, insert the Golden Curry square, ½ cup of hot water, and mix.
5. Transfer a little extra water if the sauce gets too heavy.
6. Transfer the warm rice to a container to eat and put the bits of schnitzel on board.
7. Fill with the veggies and gravy and eat immediately.

3.6 Somen Noodles with Nori Dressing

Somen pasta is extremely thin whitish Japanese white flour noodles that are often served cold. With Somen noodles as the foundation, preparing a tasty and full lunch is a snap. A savory-sweet broth spiced with soy sauce and maple syrup, light seaweed dressings, and lots of garnishes like sliced radishes, onions, shallots, and nuts make up this Somen dish. This is a popular cold noodles salad in Japan, and it is always refreshing to eat when it is hot outside. They are often served in Japanese restaurants throughout the summer. If you prefer, you may add more vinegar to the plate before you dine. The meal will be spiced up with Karashi, a Japanese fiery yellow sauce (not Dijon mustard).

Cooking Time: 1 hour

Serving Size: 2

Ingredients:

For the Noodles

- 2 packages of somen noodles

For the Seaweed Dressing

- ½ teaspoon sesame oil
- A pinch of salt
- 2-3 tablespoons sesame seeds
- 1 teaspoon sugar
- 2 sheets of nori

For the Sauce

- 2 tablespoons sesame oil
- A splash of maple syrup
- 2-3 tablespoons rice vinegar

- 2-3 tablespoons tamarind

Method:

1. Cook the pasta as per the directions provided in the box.
2. Mix all the components for the sauces and set them aside.
3. Combine and set it aside from the components for the seaweed coating.
4. Break the pasta into two cups.
5. Place over the sauces and marinade with the toppings you like. Just serve.

3.7 15-Minute Miso Soup with Greens and Tofu

This miso soup is indeed nutritious and refreshing, with a complete bunch of vegetables wilted into it. It is warm, soothing, and flavorful, with excellent tofu and seaweed pieces in every spoonful. Miso soup is a classic Japanese soup composed mostly of soy sauce, dashi (broth), veggies, seaweed, and tofu. Miso soup is usually made using a broth called "dashi," which is created by soaking seaweed like kombu in freshwater and boiling it with bonito flakes. Each taste of this soup is brimming with miso flavor and the proper amount of tofu and seaweed. In addition, each bowl has more than a full dose of greens for vegetarian fans.

Cooking Time: 15 minutes

Serving Size: 2

Ingredients:

- ½ cup chopped green onion
- ¼ cup firm tofu
- 3-4 tablespoon yellow miso

paste
- ½ cup chopped green chard
- 1 sheet nori
- 4 cups vegetable broth

Method:
1. In a small mixing bowl, put the vegetable broth and take it to a low boil.
2. Meanwhile, place the miso in a shallow saucepan (beginning from the smaller end of that scale), add a little warmer water, and swirl until soft.
3. When transferred to the broth later, this would guarantee that it does not clump. Just put it aside.
4. Transfer chard (or other vegetables of your selection), spring onions, and tofu to the liquid (insert at the end of the process, if silken is used) and cook for five minutes.
5. Insert nori, next, and mix. Add the miso solution, detach from the flame, and whisk to blend.
6. When desired, try and add additional miso or a touch of kosher salt.
7. Serve it warm. It is better when clean.

3.8 Kenchin Vegetable Soup

Kenchin jiru, also known as just kenchin, is a Traditional vegetable soup made with fresh vegetables and tofu. It is a popular Japanese meal that may be cooked in a variety of ways using a variety of ingredients. Kenchinjiru (Japanese Veggie Soup) is a transparent soup made with leafy greens, tofu, shiitake mushrooms, and wakame stock. It was originally intended as a Buddhist temple dish. If you are searching for a vegetarian supper on a chilly night, this soup is a good choice. While conventional Japanese cookery calls for a fish-based stock called "dashi," this soup is flavored with kombu and shiitake mushrooms. Although any veggies may be used, the most common components are various root vegetables. Gobo and daikon are crucial elements in the soup since they offer taste and texture.

Cooking Time: 30 minutes

Serving Size: 4

Ingredients:

- 1 tablespoon sesame oil
- ½ tablespoon oil
- 500ml boiling water
- 1 stem shallot
- ½ pack firm tofu
- 50g carrot
- 100g taro
- 125g konnyaku (½ pack)
- 50g shimeji mushrooms

- 70g daikon

Dashi Broth

- 2 tablespoon sake
- A pinch of salt
- 2 tablespoon soy sauce
- 800ml dashi stock

Method:

1. Use a paper towel to seal the tofu and position it on a flipped baking sheet.
2. On the tofu, put a tiny work surface or a jar with weights in it.
3. Leave it for another thirty minutes. Before processing the veggies, make this move.
4. Lengthwise, split konnyaku into several identical pieces.
5. Then cut each patch to 5millimeters wide parallel to the first slice.
6. A pot of hot water over the bits of konnyaku, wash.
7. Halve the squeezed tofu horizontally onto the cutting surface.
8. Cut the three sides of tofu half down the middle, then cut diagonal to the second piece to 1.5cm thick.
9. In a frying pan, add sesame seed and butter and cook over a medium temperature.
10. Place all the veggies in the pot, excluding the shallots and tofu, and cook till the vegetable parts are covered in oil.
11. Insert the tofu, then the components from Dashi Broth.

12. Set a cover on and simmer for about five minutes just until the veggies are heated through. Bring it to boiling.
13. Pull the scum from periodically while frying.
14. Transfer the shallots to the skillet, stir for fifteen seconds or so, and then switch the heat off.
15. While warm, eat.

3.9 Hearty Vegetable Miso Soup

You can make a tasty soup by combining your favorite veggies with miso. That is all there is to it! You do not need dashi or soup since the veggies are so rich in umami. It is a delicious way to appreciate seasonal veggies and a fantastic vegetarian choice. Miso-Vegetable Soup is nutrient-dense and delicious, making it an excellent lunch or light dinner option. This soothing, wholesome vegan miso soup is a hearty one-pot dinner that will nourish both the body and the spirit.

Cooking Time: 30 minutes

Serving Size: 4

Ingredients:

- 2 potatoes
- 1-2 carrots (peeled)
- 1 onion
- 5-6 mushrooms
- 2 tablespoons peanut oil
- 4 tablespoon miso paste
- 4 cups water

Method:
1. Split herbs, no bigger than ¾-inch, into small bites.
2. Sauté the vegetables in a broth sauté pan in heated oil till they become transparent; then insert the other veggies and sauté for another three minutes.
3. Add the water and cook till all veggies are tender; minimize heat to medium and insert miso paste to boil.
4. Bring to a boil and add diced leeks or cut spring onions to flavor.

3.10 Japanese Vegetable Stew with Miso Broth

A steaming bowl of soup Vegetable Miso Soup is a simple but excellent combination of comfort, health, and flavor! Japanese miso soups are also a fantastic method to integrate seasonal vegetables due to their adaptability. Miso soup is a traditional Japanese cuisine. At the very least once a day, it is on the board. When a dish of steamed rice is provided, you may anticipate miso soup to be served with it. Fortunately, preparing kombu dashi is simple. It is as easy as immersing a slice of kombu in freshwater for many hours if you can get your hands on any. You now have a vegan Kombu Dashi on your hands. You just need to boil the kombu water, then remove the kombu chunk just before boiling, and the dashi is prepared to use.

Cooking Time: 50 minutes

Serving Size: 4

Ingredients:

- 2 teaspoon soy sauce
- 2 cups dashi (stock)
- 2 tablespoon sake
- 2 tablespoon miso
- 375 grams' sweet potato
- 200 grams Napa cabbage
- 300 grams' carrots
- 1 tablespoon vegetable oil
- 200 grams' leeks
- 600 grams kabocha squash
- 4 shiitake mushrooms

Method:
1. Start preparing the dashi for 8-24 hours until you cook.
2. Keep it to use in the soup when you use entire shiitake mushrooms in the dashi.
3. Place the sweet potato in a container large enough to accommodate the squash as well.
4. Break the squash into bits the size of a bite. Place the squash along with the sweet potato in a dish.
5. Set the whites portion of the napa apart from the greenery portion.
6. Over medium pressure, heat the liquid. Insert any leeks.
7. Heat until tender, constantly stirring, for five minutes.
8. Insert the sake as well as cook, sealed, for approximately two minutes.
9. Squash and sweet potato are added. Swirl.
10. Transfer the napa cabbage and mushroom to the top part.
11. Cover and simmer for five minutes.
12. Stir in the soy sauce and turn the heat down to a low level.

3.11 Homemade Senbei Rice Crackers

Rice crackers are a popular snack in Japan, where rice is a major dietary source. Rice crackers come in two varieties in Japan: Senbei and Okaki. During the Middle Ages (789-1185), flour was used to make Chinese rice crackers (officially known as "flour crackers"). On the other hand, the Japanese were so fond of rice that they began creating crackers. That is how senbei gained popularity in Japan. Rice crackers come in various sizes, forms, and tastes (squares, rectangles, rounds, and spherical) (usually savory but sometimes sweet). You may prepare them in various methods, including baking, grilling (historically over charcoal), and deep-frying. Making Kakimochi at home is a simple technique. Simply cut mochi into small strips, let it air dry fully before breaking into pieces and deep-frying.

Cooking Time: 40 minutes

Serving Size: 4

Ingredients:
Senbei

- 2 tablespoon vegetable oil
- 4 tablespoon water
- 40g cooked white rice
- ¼ teaspoon sea salt
- 120g rice flour or mochiko

Glaze

- 2 teaspoon mirin
- 1 tablespoon soy sauce

Toppings

- 2 teaspoons red chili pepper mix

- Nori seaweed sheets
- 3 teaspoon black sesame seeds
- 5 teaspoon furikake rice

Method:

1. Preheat the oven to 190 degrees Celsius.
2. To make the glaze, whisk together the soy sauce and mirin.
3. In a mixing bowl, combine the corn starch, rice flour, salt, and oil to produce the pastry.
4. Run until the mixture is finely mixed.
5. Place the mixture in a bowl and insert your desired flavorings.
6. Remove the plastic from the dough 'disc' and place it on the prepared baking sheet.
7. Bake the pretzels for 8-10 minutes, one baking tray at a time.
8. Using a spatula, turn the pretzels.
9. Bake for 8-10 minutes more or until the crackers begin to tan.
10. Brush the soy sauce and miso glaze over the tops.
11. Return to the oven and bake for another ten minutes or until well browned.
12. Before serving, cool full on a wire rack.

Chapter 4: Japanese Vegan Recipes

4.1 Homemade Vegan Sushi Recipe

Vegan sushi cannot include any fish since it is made without the use of animal products. Fortunately, you can use so many other components to fill it that you won't miss the fish at all! This sushi recipe just requires a few materials. It is all quite simple. All of the items should be available at any average grocery shop. If you follow the directions, making delicious vegan sushi rolls is simple. Vegan sushi may be filled with a variety of ingredients. Sushi does not have to be made using fish or seafood.

Cooking Time: 50 minutes

Serving Size: 4

Ingredients:

- 1 tablespoon sugar
- 1 teaspoon of sea salt
- 4 Seaweed
- 4 cups cooked sushi rice
- 2 tablespoons rice vinegar
- Sliced cucumber

Raw Filling

- 6 sliced carrot
- 6 sliced green onion
- 6 slices cucumber
- 6 slices avocado

Cooked Filling

- 1 tablespoon Tamari soy sauce
- 1 cup sweet potato
- 1 cup Shitake mushrooms

Serving Suggestions
- Fresh pickled ginger
- Creamy peanut sauce
- Wasabi
- Tamari soy sauce

Method:
1. In a cup, add the vinegar, salt, and sugar, and steam in the oven or microwave until the sugar has melted.
2. For the cooked rice, add the combination and blend well.
3. Spilling the tamari over them while enabling them to simmer a bit as you prepare the remainder of the roll ingredients and make the brined sweet potato and mushroom.
4. For 20-30 minutes, cook at 400 degrees until crispy on the sides. Until fluffy and boiled through, you can also marinate them in a bowl.
5. Place one cup of rice onto the nori sheet to start building up.
6. In a fine line, the filling components of selection lay on one side. For every filling element, you need around 2-4 bits.
7. Do not use more than four or five ingredients for fillings, or it will become too large to roll.
8. Roll firmly and cut. Serve with spices such as Tamari for dips.

4.2 Vegan Japanese Souffle Pancakes

These Puffy Japanese Souffle Cakes taste like stringy clouds, but they are even better when topped with handmade caramel sauce and frozen strawberries! They are airy, delicate, dainty pancakes that appear a little too sophisticated for a workday breakfast but are tough to refuse on the weekends. A must-try are these velvety, silky pancakes. It is all about the eggs in Souffle Pancakes. To prepare the soufflé, split the egg whites and eggs and whip the whites. The egg whites are whisked until firm peaks form, then mixed into the remainder of the mixture softly and gently. Because the air pockets within the pancake batter keep their form, the souffle crepes are exceptionally fluffy. You could even remember the noise of air pockets escaping as you cut the cakes!

Cooking Time: 20 minutes

Serving Size: 2

Ingredients:

Dry Ingredients

- ¼ teaspoon baking soda
- Pinch of salt
- 1 tablespoon sugar
- 1 teaspoon baking powder
- 80g all-purpose flour

Wet Ingredients

- 2 teaspoons oil
- 1 teaspoon vanilla extract
- 1 tablespoon apple cider vinegar
- 80ml soy milk

Method:
1. Lubricate the appropriately with oil or vegetarian butter when you are using ring molds.
2. Mix the flour mixture very well in a pan.
3. Shift the flour mixture on one hand and insert the apple cider vinegar, vanilla extract, plant-based milk, and oil.
4. Slowly pour together all the products until no dry patches remain. Do not spill over.
5. Over the moderate fire, heat a wide skillet.
6. Transfer a thin film of oil to the rim. Turn the heat down to moderate when the oil is hot.
7. Position the molds of the ring so that among them, there seems to be some room.
8. Twice, the batter is spooned under one mold, then the other.
9. Now scoop the batter into two large piles when you are not using a mold. Use a lid to protect the pot and let it heat for ten minutes.
10. The surfaces of the cakes should never be shiny for more than ten minutes.
11. They must have some wrinkles on the horizon, and that they should appear dry on the bottom. Switch the pancakes using a spatula.
12. However, place the bowl once more and cook for the next three minutes before the pancakes are cooked fully.
13. Remove and expose the bowl from the flame.
14. Serve with a vegetarian oil or a coconut whip and golden syrup instantly.

4.3 Japanese Vegan Pancakes Dorayaki with Red Bean Filling

Dorayaki is a traditional Japanese sweet. It comprises 2 little castella pancake-like burgers folded around a sweet azuki beans puree filling. There was just one layer in the classic Dorayaki. Usagiya in Japan's Ueno area came up with the present design in 1914. Dorayaki is a delicious red bean filling sandwiched between two honey pancakes. In Japan, it is very popular with both children and adults. If you are acquainted with 1970s Japanese cartoons, you are acquainted with this dish thanks to the animated character Doraemon, who is obsessed with them and jumps for any trick surrounding them.

Cooking Time: 20 minutes

Serving Size: 2

Ingredients:

- Vegetable oil
- ½ cup red bean paste
- 2 tablespoon mirin or maple syrup
- ¼ teaspoon soy sauce
- ½ cup sifted cake flour
- 2 teaspoon baking powder
- ⅓ cup soy milk
- 2 tablespoon powdered sugar

Method:

1. In a large cup, mix the flour, icing sugar, and cornstarch.

2. Add the maple syrup, soy milk, and soy sauce to some other dish.

3. To form a delicious mixture, drop the dried mixture into the wet one, and mix.

4. It is not meant to be so dense, but this should be small enough just to pour. For ten minutes, let everything sit.

5. In a non-stick pan or pot, pour that small amount of oil and warm it over moderate flame.

6. To disperse the oil equally, use a towel. You just want the slightest amount to help shade the pancakes but not adhere to them.

7. Reduce heat to medium, and dump about two tablespoons of the batter in as ideal the round as you can find on the non-stick plate.

8. You need all of them to be approximately the same number.

9. For around two minutes, heat on the first hand, bubbles might rise on edge, and the sides will cook very easily.

10. For around one more minute, turn and heat on the other hand.

11. Enable your cakes to chill for several minutes, then add a dollop of Anko, the bean paste, to each of them.

12. To make the Dorayaki, cover it with a croissant and stack it all together.

13. Serve with a swirl of icing sugar or cream cheese or diced strawberries with almond.

4.4 Vegan Poke Bowl

Poke is a meal made of sliced raw fish that may be served as an appetizer or a main meal. It is one of the most popular meals in Native Hawaiian culture. Aku and hee is the characteristic patterns. Except in regions like Niihau, where the Hawaiian dialect is spoken, hee poke is normally referred to by its Japanese name, tako poked. Egan is a fictional character. Poke Bowl (also known as Tofu Poke Bowl) is a fast and simple lunch bowl made with soft tofu and onions cooked in a tasty ginger-soy sauce and served with rice, red cabbage, cucumbers, and avocados. Tofu poke plates are a quick and nutritious lunch, supper, or make-ahead dish that can be made in about 20 minutes. The brilliance of this Poke Bowl Food is that it can be made in any way you like.

Cooking Time: 20 minutes

Serving Size: 2

Ingredients:

For Pan-Fried Tofu

- ½ tablespoon rice vinegar
- 1 teaspoon chili paste (Sambal Oelek)
- 1 tablespoon sesame oil (roasted)
- 3 tablespoon soy sauce
- 1 block fried firm tofu
- ⅛ onion

For Vegan Poke Bowl

- ½ teaspoon sesame seeds
- ½ teaspoon white sesame seeds
- 2 cups cooked brown rice

- 2 tablespoon shelled edamame
- 1 carrot
- ¼ English cucumber
- ½ avocado
- 1 lime
- ½ watermelon radish
- 2 green onions
- ⅛ red cabbage

Method:
1. Collect all the components.
2. Start cooking the veggies next if you want to make delicious tofu, and come back to this phase later. Instead of that, cut the white onion finely.
3. Open and extract all moisture from the tofu packet.
4. Break the tofu, about twelve bits, into bite-sized bits.
5. Then warm the sesame oil across moderate heat in a large cooking pan and add the large onion.
6. Sauté once oil covers the onions. Insert the blocks of tofu next.
7. Insert Rice Vinegar, soy sauce, and sambal oelek as soon as the tofu is covered with oil.
8. Decrease the oven temperature and cover the liquid with the tofu.
9. Switch off the fire and, when the tofu is well-coated with the liquid, extract it from the stove.
10. Break the carrot into specific shapes and then slice it into pieces of julienne.

11. Take the skin of the cucumber, leave a portion unpeeled and slice it into small strips.
12. Chop the radish from the watermelon and slice it into small pieces.
13. Break the green cabbage's tough heart and slice finely.
14. Trim the spring onions horizontally into a thin slice.
15. Chop the avocado softly and cut it into ½ inch strips.
16. Break the avocado into pieces, then. To keep it from overcooking, split the lime in two and pour the juice over the avocado.
17. In two big pots, prepare the fried brown rice.
18. First, put the weighty vegetables, such as avocado, fry tofu, and red cabbage.
19. The remainder of the components is then added.
20. Spray the end with sesame seeds and spring onions.

4.5 Japanese Vegan Udon Noodle Soup

Udon noodles, a mainstay of Asian food, have captivated the affections and stomachs of foodies all over the globe. These rich, silky, and satisfying wheat noodles are often seen in stews, even without animal-based foods, but always accompanied by thin slices of veggies, mirin, soy, garlic powder, and ginger, as well as the essential umami taste provided by mushrooms. Chinese cabbage, onions, green onions, and peanuts are used in this vegetarian version of this Japanese-inspired soup. It is comparable to a classic dish, so it'll keep you warm and fill you up without being too heavy. This udon soup is a simple way to taste traditional Japanese tastes and a tasty light lunch or supper.

Cooking Time: 25 minutes

Serving Size: 4

Ingredients:

For the Broth

- Salt
- Pepper
- 2 tablespoons mushroom sauce
- ½ teaspoon chili paste
- 2 tablespoons rice vinegar
- ¼ cup soy sauce
- 4 cups vegetable broth
- 1 pinch sugar
- 2 pieces ginger

For Assembling

- ¼ cup cilantro (chopped)
- ½ cup peanuts
- 4 medium green onions
- 1 pound udon noodles

For the Chinese Broccoli

- 2 tablespoons sesame oil
- 1 pound Chinese broccoli
- ½ tablespoon ginger
- 2 cloves garlic
- 1 tablespoon peanut oil

Method:

1. Collect components.
2. Mix the veggie broth or vegan chicken stock with spice, rice vinegar, sugar, mushroom sauce, soy sauce, and chili paste in a small saucepan.
3. To mix, swirl to get to a boil. Turn down the heat and let it boil to a simmer.
4. Enable at least ten minutes for the liquid to boil.
5. Take from the stock the bits of spice and dispose of them. With pepper and salt, dress gently.
6. Warm the sunflower oil in a different medium saucepan and insert minced garlic, ginger, and sesame oil.
7. For two or three minutes, let that be citrusy and add the minced Chinese kale.
8. Sauté for several moments, till the broccoli is just soft and the color is light green.
9. Cover and set it aside from the fire.

10. Put a portion of pasta in each, preparing individual cups, top it with the Chinese kale packed, a healthy portion of soup, some chopped spring onions, minced cilantro, and unsalted almonds.

4.6 Vegan Nabe (Hot Pot with Miso)

Miso paste, which is being used as the major flavor to the basis of dashi soup, is one of the important components for this noodle soup, as the name implies. Vegetables like napa cabbage, green leafy vegetables, and thinly sliced pork are then put to the stir fry to roast and enjoy the ponzu sauces. Soy milk hot pot is offered in tofu eateries and ryokan and is intended to be a communal meal where family and friends gather around the table to enjoy the dish. The broth has a lovely taste to it. Everything blends when all the veggies and seasonings are immersed in the broth, culminating in a well-rounded, flavorful hot pot.

Cooking Time: 40 minutes

Serving Size: 4

Ingredients:

- 4 cups water
- Salt, to taste
- 2 pieces of kombu
- 4 Shiitake Mushrooms
- 1 handful Enoki mushrooms
- ½ Napa cabbage
- 1 handful Mizuna greens
- 2 tablespoons white miso paste
- 1 leek, sliced

- 1 dried chili pepper
- 1 tablespoon soy sauce
- 1 turnip, sliced thinly
- 1 small carrot, sliced

Method:
1. Add the water, shiitake mushrooms, leeks, kombu, turnip, carrot, chili pepper, and soy sauce to the pot.
2. For thirty minutes, carry to a light boil.
3. Meanwhile, insert the miso in a small container and pour a few cups of water once it becomes a dense sauce texture.
4. This would make the blending of the broth simpler.
5. Switch off the heating after thirty minutes.
6. If required, mix in the miso paste and salts and insert the mizuna, cabbage, and enoki mushroom.
7. Instantly serve.

4.7 Japanese-Style Katsudon Rice Bowls

Tonkatsu (baked, deep-fried meat) and eggs are simmered in a salty and sweet soup and eaten over rice in katsudon, a traditional Japanese meal. In Japanese, katsu, or "fillet," alludes to the meat that has been pressed thin before being fried. This is a bowl meal known as don or donburi. Compared to other donburi, katsudon is heavy, but the flavor is so wonderful that you won't mind the additional calories from deep-frying the tonkatsu. Katsudon is regarded as southern food in Japanese culture, representing a delightful warm dinner that can thaw even the coldest portion of your heart. Katsudon is a traditional Japanese lunch meal that may be found at various informal eateries, including udon noodle shops, tiny corner eateries, and bento shops.

Cooking Time: 40 minutes

Serving Size: 2

Ingredients:

Tofu Katsu

- Chopped spring onions
- Sesame seeds
- Neutral oil for frying
- 2-3 cups steamed Japanese rice
- 1 200g block extra firm tofu
- 1 red onion thinly sliced
- ¼ teaspoon salt

Batter

- ½ teaspoon sea salt
- ¼ cup room temperature water
- ½ teaspoon baking powder

- ½ tablespoon cornstarch
- ¼ cup all-purpose flour

Breading

- ½ cup Japanese bread crumbs

Sauce

- 2 tablespoon cane sugar
- 2 tablespoon soy sauce
- 3 dried shiitake mushrooms

Method:

1. For the paste, wash the dried mushrooms in warm water for five to ten minutes.
2. Do not dispose of the liquid. Cut and put the mushrooms back.
3. Use a tofu push or cover it in a paper towel liquid from the tofu and then place a heavy solid surface (a panel or tray) on the edge.
4. Leave it for fifteen minutes till the towels have drained the sweat.
5. Break the tofu into rectangular bricks ½-inch thick.
6. Determines the thickness of the tofu, you will be able to break one tofu into three slabs. Dress with ¼ teaspoon of salt.
7. By stirring all the components until creamy, cook the mixture.
8. Add the breadcrumbs to another sheet or plate.
9. Put each tofu in the mixture and then cover the breadcrumbs with it. Repeat the process here.
10. In a cooking pot, warm the oil. Once heated, throw in the tofu.

11. Fry on medium-high heat for about eight minutes, turning halfway, till both sides are nicely browned.

12. Remove the tofu from the butter and then turn the heat down.

13. Allow cool for fifteen minutes, then cut into ¾ inch thick slices horizontally.

14. Take the butter from the pot cautiously.

15. Insert the mushroom broth, mushrooms, and garlic, and cook for three minutes.

16. Put in the sugars and soy sauce. Combine well and boil till the sugar dissolves.

17. Insert the diced katsu tofu.

18. Use a spoon to gently pick the sauces and spill the tofu until it is well covered.

19. Allow to steam until nearly all the fluid has been drained by the tofu. Switch the heat off.

20. Put the tofu over all the Japanese fried rice. Feel free to flavor, if necessary, with some green onions and pumpkin seeds.

4.8 Japanese Coco Ichibanya-Style Vegetable Curry

The British brought curries to Japan in the late 1800s, and it was initially made out of Western-style stews blended with curry powder. Soon after that, they modified Japanese curry to their form, Curry Rice. S&B Products began selling curry sauce in the form of blocks in the 1950s, and anybody could prepare it at home. This veggie-packed meal is kid-friendly and delicious, with sweet and salty flavors that will have everyone clamoring for seconds. One of the all-time favorite comfort meals is Japanese curry. Coco Ichibanya is a well-known Japanese restaurant chain specializing in kare raisu (Japanese for curry rice). You may personalize your curry by selecting the amount of spice, flavor intensity, rice quantity, ingredients, and garnishes that make this restaurant stand out. It might not be easy to choose the right curry sauce mix when there are so many options.

Cooking Time: 55 minutes

Serving Size: 6

Ingredients:

- 1 box Japanese curry roux mix
- Cooked Japanese rice
- 1 Japanese eggplant
- 8 cherry tomatoes
- 2 tablespoons vegetable oil
- 1 thumb-size fresh ginger
- 2 medium potatoes

- 1 ½ cup green beans
- 1 apple
- 5 cups water
- 1 large carrot
- 1 large onion

Method:

1. Drain in ice water the sliced eggplant and keep for fifteen minutes. Some of the bitterness will be removed from this.
2. Transfer 1 tablespoon oil, grated ginger, and apples to a big saucepan over moderate heat.
3. Insert the onions and roast for three minutes, just until the pieces are transparent and tender.
4. Incorporate liquid and mix. Insert the green beans, carrot, and potatoes and mix.
5. For three minutes, fry on each hand, once crispy and soft.
6. Turn the heat down and shift it to a sheet lined with a clean cloth. Just put it aside.
7. Put the lid on again and boil for the remaining two minutes.
8. Serve with fukujinzuke and Japanese fried rice.

4.9 Spicy Vegetarian Ramen Gyoza

This ramen base is very creamy and thick, and it can fool you into believing it is Tonkotsu. In Japanese, soy milk noodles are not always vegan or vegetarian. The broth may be produced using pig bone or poultry carcass, like ordinary Tonkotsu, Eel sauce, or Miso soup. Most ramen soups include a seafood-based broth made with bonito particles and kelp to add to the soup's complexity. Use dashi, powdered shiitake mushrooms, and wakame to make this recipe vegan and vegetarian.

Cooking Time: 1 hour

Serving Size: 4

Ingredients:

- 4 baby bok choy
- 4 5-oz. packages ramen noodles
- 3 tablespoons unsalted butter
- 1 tablespoon soy sauce
- 4 garlic cloves
- 8 dried shiitake mushrooms
- 1 piece dried kombu
- ¼ cup vegetable oil
- 1 2" piece ginger
- 2 tablespoon tomato paste
- 1 tablespoon black sesame seeds
- Kosher salt
- 4 scallions
- 1 tablespoon. gochugaru

Method:

1. Cook the garlic and ¼ cup of the oil in a medium saucepan over medium heat, frequently whisking, until the garlic is translucent, around four minutes.
2. Heat the remaining two tablespoons of oil to moderate in the preserved pot.
3. Insert the tomato sauce and simmer for about two minutes, stirring regularly, before it appears to adhere to the sides of the pan and blackens gradually.
4. Insert the Kombu and mushroom, then whisk in five cups of cold water.
5. Move the solids to a mixer using a rubber spatula.
6. To mix, add a spoonful or two of liquid and purée until creamy.
7. Add oil a slice at a time, until introducing more, whisking to mix with each addition.
8. In the meantime, put it to a boil with a big pot of water. Insert bok choy and cook for about two minutes until it is greenish and soft.

4.10 Japanese Miso Eggplant

This dish is one of the easiest and most delicious ways to cook the nightshade vegetable if you like eggplant. You may use either Japanese or China eggplants with a long, thin body for this recipe. Cut the eggplants in half to make boat-like pieces, then slice them to soak the umami soy combination. To bake, just place them in the oven at the broil temperature and bake until the outside is slightly browned and the inside is creamy. It has a sweet, salty, and savory taste. This eggplant meal is so delicious that even vegetarians will like it. This roasted miso-coated eggplant dish has a caramelized crispy top and a creamy inside, making it an eggplant lover's fantasy.

Cooking Time: 30 minutes

Serving Size: 4

Ingredients:

- 80g white miso paste
- Black sesame seeds
- 1 tablespoon sesame oil
- 1 teaspoon finely ginger
- 2 tablespoons raw sugar
- 1 tablespoon Shaoxing wine
- 2 tablespoons mirin
- 2 tablespoons cooking sake
- Pinch of sea salt flakes
- 4 black eggplants

Method:
1. Heat the oven to 200C.

2. Clean the eggplants, then wipe them dry. Break the eggplants, width-wise, in two.
3. Rate a diamond shape on the eggplant's surface and use a paring blade as seen in the images.
4. Let it sit for thirty minutes.
5. Shake off any particles of salts that remain.
6. In a tiny, hard bottom frying pan, put the Shaoxing wine, mirin, sugar, sake, ginger, sesame oil, and miso paste on low.
7. Cook for thirty minutes in the well-heated oven until golden and soft.
8. Spray with sesame oil and eat warm with coconut rice and daikon.

Conclusion

Without a doubt, Japan has become one of the world's great food countries. New seasonal harvest and gentle preparation are the key components of Japanese cuisine. Japanese cuisine has exploded into the culinary scene. It is no surprise that Japanese cuisine is so common, given its mastery of flavors and delicate balance of sweet and savory. Japanese and Japanese-inspired foods can be found worldwide, even in the local kitchen, mainly seafood and ramen. Water is also at the heart of Japanese food, with dashi made from Kombu (kelp) and bonito particles in water serving as the basis for all Japanese sauces. The essence of Japanese cuisine is new, seasonal flavors cooked simply in water. As a result, it carries the "healthy" label well. Wasabi is among the globe's most challenging ingredients to produce, and that is why the crop is so pricey. Many wasabis in cafes are usually horseradish combined with food dye processing for this purpose. True wasabi has a more herbal taste than the artificial type, but it lacks its punch for about fifteen minutes after being diced. A component of Japanese food is rice. It is also popular to eat rice cakes (mochi). They vary from savory to sweet and have many different methods, from grilled to boil. With heavy effects from both Korea and China, Japanese cuisine has been around for more than centuries. And it is only been several decades before all the results of what is now recognized as Japanese cuisine has begun to exist. Currently, the four seasons and climate also have a significant influence on Japanese food. Most frequently, fish and veggies are consumed. Although the food may sound almost ordinary to some western people, tastiness, appearance, and combination of flavors are of utmost importance. This book has all types of Japanese dishes categorizing into breakfast, snacks, lunch, dinner, soups, and some of the famous recipes of Japanese cuisine.

Try these recipes and start preparing your easy and delicious Japanese meals.

Printed in Great Britain
by Amazon